JOURNEY THROUGH
INDIA

ANITA GANERI

FRANKLIN WATTS
LONDON • SYDNEY

Franklin Watts
First published in Great Britain in 2016 by The Watts Publishing Group

Credits
Editor in Chief: John C. Miles
Series Editor: Amy Stephenson
Series Designer: Emma DeBanks
Picture Researcher: Diana Morris

Picture Credits: Anandoart/Dreamstime: 7tr, 23b. Antonella865/Dreamstime: 14b. Ken Bacher Dreamstime: 7c, 7bla. Sergey Chernov/Dreamstime: 1. Chrisadby/Dreamstime: 24. Rafal Cichawa/Dreamstime: 6c, 16-17. Adrian Constantinescu/Dreamstime: 8. dbimages/Alamy: 7br, 28c. Dinodia Photos/Alamy: 9bc. Piotr Furman/Dreamstime: 29cr. Ganesh4photolife/Dreamstime: 26. Kirat Grewal/Dreamstime: 6tr. Jorg Hachemann/Dreamstime: 14c, 15t. Trini Jacobs/Dreamstime: 27t. Kishore Jothady/Dreamstime: 9t. JTB Photo/Alamy: 18. Milino Kefkar/Dreamstime: 7tllbc, 15c. Denis Kelly/Dreamstime: 13c. Vadim Kulikov/Dreamstime: 21t. Shawn Low/Dreamstime: 23t. Lunamarina/Dreamstime: 6br. Gaurav Masand/Dreamstime: 25c. Zoenek Matyás/Dreamstime: 4. Alexander Mazurkevich/Shutterstock: 11t. Aliaksandr Mazurkevich/Dreamstime: 6bc, 19t. Mcherevan/Dreamstime: 6cr. Simon Montgomery/Alamy: 17br. Luciano Mortula/Dreamstime: 12-13. David Munden/Popperfoto/Getty Images: 21b. Klaus Nahr wikimedia commons: 29cl. Marina Pissarova/Dreamstime: 7tlb. Purepix/Alamy: 20. Radiokafka/Shutterstock: 5t. Radius Images/Alamy: 19b. Simon Reddy/Alamy: 6tl, 9br. Dmitry Rukhlenko/Dreamstime: 11b. Samrat35/Dreamstime: 22. Lena Serditova/Shutterstock: 10c. Sommai Sommai/Dreamstime: 7ca. Nickolay Stanev/Dreamstime: 5b. Kieran Stavan/wikimedia commons: 25b. Stockshooter/Dreamstime: 28-29. Szefei/Dreamstime: 7tl. Theskaman306/Shutterstock: 13b. Richard Thomas/Dreamstime: 7cra. Travel Pictures/Alamy: 27b. Harish Tyagi/EPA Alamy: 3, 15b. Videowokart Dreamstime: 7cr. Xiaofeng Wang/Dreamstime: 7bl. wikimedia commons: 10b. WisconsinArt/Dreamstime: 7cl. Yulia Yurasova/Dreamstime: 16b. Vladimir Zhuravlev/Dreamstime: front cover, 7crb, 25tl.

Dewey number: 954.0532
HB ISBN: 978 1 4451 3678 3

Printed in Malaysia

Franklin Watts
An imprint of
Hachette Children's Group
Part of The Watts Publishing Group
Carmelite House
50 Victoria Embankment
London EC4Y 0DZ

An Hachette UK Company
www.hachette.co.uk

www.franklinwatts.co.uk

CONTENTS

WELCOME TO INDIA!

Bharat mein aapka swaagat hai! Welcome to India! Covering an area of around 3,287,600 sq km, the Republic of India is the world's seventh largest country. It is also a fascinating place – vast and colourful, with an extraordinary variety of people, landscapes, languages (including Hindi, above), religions and culture. It would take years to cover all of India in one journey, so this trip takes in some of the country's many highlights, whisking you from desert forts to bustling cities to tranquil tea plantations – and much, much more!

Indian landscapes

Located in South Asia, India is so big that it forms a sub-continent with Bangladesh and Pakistan. Fringed in the south by the Indian Ocean, which includes the Bay of Bengal and the Arabian Sea, it is bordered to the north by the mighty Himalayas, a range that boasts nine of the ten highest mountains on Earth. Across India, landscapes and climate vary enormously. On your journey, you'll visit meandering rivers, sandy deserts, tropical backwaters, and fabulous beaches. The climate ranges from alpine and temperate in the north to tropical in the south. And watch out for the summer monsoon when it can rain every day for weeks on end.

▼ The towering Himalayas in the north are a dramatic range of snow-capped peaks.

► Busy Indian streets, like this one in Kolkata, are full of pedestrians, colourful buses and auto rickshaws.

Story of India

India has a long and rich history. Around 2500 BCE, the Indus Valley Civilisation flourished in the north-west, in what is now Pakistan. Since then, many different peoples and cultures have left their mark. In the 16th–18th centuries, much of India was ruled by the Mughals – Muslims from the north-west. In the 18th century, India came under British rule – a time known as the British Raj. After many revolts and wars against British rule – including the 'Quit India' movement that was led by Mahatma Gandhi (1869–1948) – India won independence in 1947. It was split into two countries, India (mainly Hindu) and Pakistan (mainly Muslim).

Indian life

More than 1.2 billion people live in India, making it the second most populated country in the world and the world's largest democracy. Hundreds of languages are spoken, and the way people live across this vast region varies enormously. In general, though, Indian people are very family-focused. Many live in large families with several generations – grandparents, parents and children – all sharing the same home.

Kya aap Hindi bolte hain?

Do you speak Hindi? Hindi and English are the official languages of India. Here are a few useful Hindi phrases to help you on your journey.

Namaste – hello
Haan – yes/thank you
Nahin – no
Koi baat nahi – no problem
Aap kaise hain? – how are you?
Aapka naam kya hai? – what is your name?
Main Hindi nahin bolta hoon – I don't speak Hindi

▲ Many signs in India are in more than one language.

PAKISTAN

NEPAL

INDIA

BANGLADESH

MYANMAR

Arabian Sea

Bay of Bengal

N
E
S

Indian
Ocean

SRI LANKA

YOUR JOURNEY

1

KEY

——— your route
around India

------- flight

——— river

——— road

★ capital city

Kargil
Leh
ritsar
Shimla
Chandigarh

TIBET

④

CHINA

NEW DELHI
NEPAL
amuna
iver
River
Ganges
Bareilly
hpur Sikri
Lucknow
Agra
aipur
Kanpur
Gorakhpur
Gwalior
③
Varanasi
ota
Allahabad
Patna

*Mount
Khangehendzonga*
Himalayas
Darjeeling
Bagdogra
Gangtok
Siliguri
Itanagar
Tinsukia
Dibrugarh
Dispur
Kohima
Shillong
Silchar
④
Imphal
BANGLADESH

Bhopal
Jabalpur
Jamshedpur
Agartala
Aizawl

Kolkata
Haldia
ndore
Raipur
MYANMAR
Nagpur
Balasore

Hyderabad
Visakhapatnam
Kakinada
Paradip
Bhubaneswar

⑤

Guntakal
Bay of Bengal

Bangalore
Chennai
Mahabalipuram
Pondicherry
Cuddalore
Coimbatore

⑥

Andaman Sea

⑤ Madurai
leppy
Rameswaram
Tuticorin
SRI LANKA
Trivandrum

ARRIVING IN MUMBAI

▲ Morning and evening, commuters crowd into Mumbai's stations.

Your journey starts in Mumbai, on the west coast. The capital of the state of Maharashtra, it is the most crowded city in India, teeming with some 20 million people. It is also India's financial centre and home to Asia's oldest stock exchange, as well as industries as diverse as IT and textiles. There are many ways of reaching Mumbai – by plane, train, car or bus. To make a grand entrance, arrive by train at the Chhatrapati Shivaji Terminus. Built in 1887, this impressive railway station is an extravaganza of arches, spires and domes. More than one thousand trains and two million passengers pass through the station every day.

Gateway to India

From the station, take a taxi or bus to the Gateway of India (see right), Mumbai's most famous landmark. For travellers arriving from Britain by ship during the British Raj, this monument was their first sight of India. It was built to mark the visit of the British monarchs, King George V and Queen Mary in 1911, and it looks very impressive at night when it is lit up. From here, hop on a ferry for a day trip to Elephanta Island, with its amazing cave temples and three-headed statue of the Hindu god, Shiva, carved out of the rock.

Mumbai life

Mumbai is a lively and noisy city. There are crowds of people everywhere and it is easy for visitors to get lost. The city's *dabbawallas*, however, know the chaotic streets like the backs of their hands. They collect freshly cooked lunches from thousands of homes and deliver them to office workers across the city. Incredibly, the lunches hardly ever get lost or delivered to the wrong person. Mumbai – like much of India – is also a city of contrasts. There are millions of well-off people who live here, but it is also home to India's largest slum, and beggars and street children are a common sight.

Seaside strolls

Mumbai is built on a long, narrow promontory, jutting out into the Arabian Sea. The sea is vital to life in Mumbai. The city is home to India's busiest international port, and in the evenings, crowds of people stroll along the coast via Marine Drive, enjoying the sunset and a refreshing drink of coconut water.

► A dabbawalla's cart packed with lunches for hungry Mumbai workers.

Bollywood

Mumbai is the home of the Indian film industry, nicknamed 'Bollywood'. Hundreds of films are made here every year, and the films contribute millions of Indian rupees to India's economy. Every day, millions of Indians go to the cinema to see the latest films. The films are blockbusters starring superstar actors and actresses. They are packed with singing, dancing and action, often lasting for several hours.

◄ Posters advertising Bollywood films.

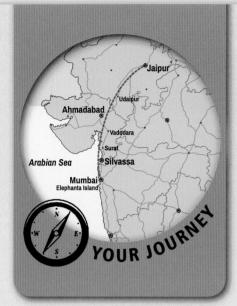

MUMBAI TO JAIPUR

From Mumbai, the quickest way to reach Jaipur in the north-west is by plane, and the journey takes just under 2 hours. A taxi will take you from the airport into the city. Jaipur's streets are chaotic so be prepared to sit in a traffic jam for a while! But it is well worth it. Jaipur is called the 'Pink City', after its pink-washed buildings. It's a fascinating place to explore. There are plenty of sightseeing tours available, by bus or car – just ask at the tourist office.

Things to see in Jaipur

Hawa Mahal (see right) – Built in 1799 for the *Maharaja* (an Indian ruler or king), the name of this beautiful building means 'Palace of the Winds'. Its high wall was designed to catch the breeze and cool the people sitting inside.

Jantar Mantar – Built in the early 18th century, this astronomical observatory has 19 huge instruments, including the world's largest stone sundial.

Johari Bazaar – A road lined with traditional shops, selling everything from jewellery to carpets. If you want to pick up a bargain, be ready to haggle over the price.

Elephant Festival – Held every year (usually in March) during the festival of Holi (festival of colour). Elephants are paraded through the streets wearing brightly-coloured paint, cloths and jewellery.

World Trade Park – Jaipur's not all about history. Take a look at Jaipur's thoroughly modern shopping, office and entertainment complex (see right).

'Land of Kings'

Jaipur is the capital of Rajasthan, which means the Land of Kings. It is a state rich in royal history, with magnificent forts, fairytale palaces, beautiful temples and stunning scenery, including the vast Thar Desert. As Rajasthan is so big, a good way to get around is to buy a ticket for the 'Palace on Wheels', a luxury train that visits the historic cities of Jaipur, Jodhpur, Jaisalmer and Udaipur. On board, as its name suggests, you will be treated like a king or queen!

Hilltop forts

Perched high on the hills around Jaipur are dramatic forts that once guarded the city. The most famous is Amer Fort, which was completed at the end of the 16th century. You can climb up to the fort's entrance or take a ride on an elephant. Once inside, head for the 'Sheesh Mahal' – a room decorated with tiny mirrors that glint in the light. Then enjoy the stunning views over the lake below. Look out for the star-shaped flower beds in the exquisite gardens that were once planted with saffron crocuses. Saffron is a very expensive spice that is used extensively in Indian cuisine.

▼ Elephant rides to and from the Amer Fort take visitors through the main entrance, which is called the 'Sun Gate'.

▼ Camels are adapted to survive in Rajasthan's dry environment. They are also a popular way to see the sights of the Thar Desert.

11

TO

Agra, home to the
train or deluxe
drive the 230 km
d – Indian roads
cks, camel carts
n, people don't
ire a car with a
ds!

Taj Mahal

In the 16th and 17th centuries, Agra was the capital of the mighty Mughal Empire. Using craftsmen from Persia and Central Asia, the Mughal emperors built beautiful forts, palaces and tombs. The most famous of these is the Taj Mahal. It was built by Emperor Shah Jahan (1592–1666) as a tomb for his wife, Mumtaz, who died in 1631. The Taj Mahal is built from white marble from Rajasthan, and inlaid with semi-precious stones from all over Asia. It took 20,000 workers 12 years to complete and 3 million people visit it every year!

Fatehpur Sikri

From Agra, take a short drive to another spectacular Mughal city – Fatehpur Sikri. Built by Emperor Akbar (1542–1605), it was his capital from 1571–85, but was then abandoned because of a lack of water. Take a guided tour around the ghostly sandstone buildings of Akbar and his court, including the Hiran Minar, a memorial to the emperor's favourite elephant. Then tie a cotton thread on the screen around the tomb of the holy man, Salim Chishti (1478–1572), and make a wish. Legend says that it will come true.

▶ Many Muslims celebrate the holy festival of Eid at Fatehpur Sikri.

Holy water

The Taj Mahal stands on the bank of the River Yamuna, the largest tributary of the River Ganges. The Ganges and the Yamuna provide water for millions of people who live along them and their floodplains. Both rivers are considered to be sacred. Every three years, millions of pilgrims gather to bathe in the water where the Ganges, Yamuna and Sarasvati rivers meet. They believe that bathing in the rivers will wash away their wrong-doings.

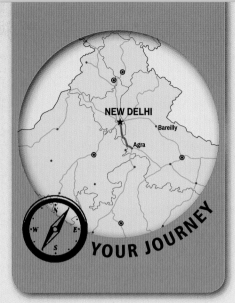

YOUR JOURNEY

AGRA TO NEW DELHI

You could take a 2-day boat trip along the Yamuna from Agra to New Delhi. However, India has one of the largest railway networks in the world, with around 115,000 km of track and more than 7,000 stations. More than 23 million people travel by train every day, so why not join them? Trains run regularly between Agra and New Delhi, but you'll need to book in advance to avoid the queues.

▼ Visitors to the Red Fort taking a rest close to its towering walls.

About New Delhi

New Delhi is the capital of India and it is a huge city of around 13 million people. As you would expect it is a vibrant mix of old and new, with modern industries like IT and the media, and glittering sporting venues alongside historic buildings and poverty-stricken slums.

New Delhi has played an important part in Indian history and there are a huge number of sights to see, from the Red Fort built by the Mughals, to the grand parliament buildings built in 1927. New Delhi is also home to the National Museum and the Raj Ghat, a memorial that marks the spot where the great Indian leader, Mahatma Gandhi, was cremated in 1948.

◀ The fresh flowers on the Raj Ghat are put there every day by volunteers.

Getting about

To get around New Delhi, hire a car and driver, or hop into an auto rickshaw. Alternatively, try Delhi's Metro (see right), which has six lines running all over the city – you can buy a special Tourist Card. For a very different experience, book onto a DelhiByCycle tour. There are five routes available, taking in all the main sights and a tour guide will help you navigate the busy streets.

Republic Day

If you're in New Delhi on 26 January, head to the *Rajpath* (King's Way) for the annual Republic Day Parade. It marks the date on which India became a republic in 1950, and is a national holiday. Regiments from India's armed forces – some mounted on camels – together with schoolchildren and ceremonial elephants, march down this wide boulevard, past the President of India. There are also colourful floats, representing the country's different states.

▲ Spectators watch a parade float that represents the state of Goa during a Republic Day Parade.

▶ Jalebi are traditionally a circular shape.

Delhi street food

Delhi's street food is both famous and delicious – here are a few favourites.

Chhole bhatura – spiced chickpeas and puffy fried bread

Papri chaat – fried bread, served with potatoes, chickpeas, yoghurt and tamarind chutney

Bhutta – roasted corn on the cob

Golgappas – crispy fried dough balls, filled with vegetables, spices and tamarind water

Kulle – hollowed-out fruit, filled with spices, chickpeas and pomegranate seeds

Lassi – a sweet or salty creamy yoghurt drink

Jalebi – crispy fried batter rings in syrup

Kulfi – Indian ice cream

NEW DELHI TO CHANDIGARH

A short flight takes you from New Delhi to Amritsar, your next stop. It's about 460 km north-west of New Delhi, in the state of Punjab. The name 'Punjab' means 'the land of five rivers' and most of the state lies in a river floodplain. The soil here is very rich, and Punjab is known as the granary of India, producing huge amounts of wheat and rice, along with cotton, sugarcane and corn.

▶ The Golden Temple sits in the centre of a large, square 'tank' filled with holy water. The water comes from the nearby River Ravi.

Sikh religion

Punjab is the home of the Sikh religion, which was begun in 1499 by a holy man called Guru Nanak. Today, more than half of Punjabis are Sikhs. Sikhs worship in temples called gurdwaras, in front of their sacred book, the Guru Granth Sahib. Traditionally, Sikhs wear five signs of their faith, known as the Five Ks. These are: *Kesh* (uncut hair), *Kangha* (wooden comb), *Kirpan* (dagger), *Kara* (steel bangle) and *Kachera* (white undershorts).

▶ A young Sikh man observing the Five Ks. His hair, comb and shorts are not visible, but the steel bangle and dagger can be clearly seen.

Golden Temple

The main reason for heading to Amritsar is to visit the spectacular Golden Temple, the Sikhs' holiest site. Built from marble, and covered in copper and gold, it was designed by the fifth Sikh Guru, Arjan (1563–1606). Its four doors symbolise the openness of the Sikh religion to all. As a sign of respect, take off your shoes and cover your head before you enter. Inside, you can listen to the temple musicians singing verses from the Guru Granth Sahib. Afterwards, all visitors are given a free meal of *dahl* (lentil stew) and bread from the temple kitchens. The kitchen serves thousands of meals every day.

Modern city

From Amritsar, hop on a superfast express train to Chandigarh, the capital of Punjab and the wealthiest city in India. The journey takes about 4 hours. This very modern-looking city was designed in the 1950s by the famous Swiss-French architect, Le Corbusier (1887–1965). It is laid out on a grid that is divided into 57 blocks. Go for a sail on Sukhna Lake or visit the Rock Garden and its amazing sculptures, which are made from waste metal and pottery. Then stop for a picnic in the Rose Garden, which has more than 1,600 types of roses.

▼ The 'Open Hand Monument' was also designed by Le Corbusier. It is a symbol of Chandigarh's government.

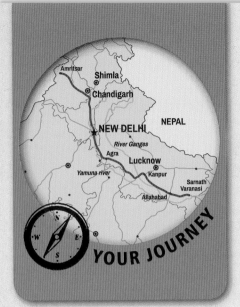

YOUR JOURNEY

CHANDIGARH TO VARANASI

The next leg of your journey takes you by car along a stretch of the Grand Trunk Road, which runs for around 2,500 km from Bangladesh in the east, across northern India, to Afghanistan in the west. Pick up the road near Chandigarh where it forms the modern road NH-2. Your destination is Varanasi, around 795 km away. The drive takes around 12 hours, so you may want to stop off overnight at Kanpur or Allahabad.

Holy city

For the first-time visitor, Varanasi can seem an overwhelming place. It is noisy, colourful, crowded – and fascinating! Located on the banks of the River Ganges, Varanasi is one of the holiest cities for Hindus. Millions of pilgrims visit every year to bathe in the river. They believe that the water will wash away their sins. They also visit the city's temples, many of which are dedicated to the god Shiva, who chose Varanasi as his home on Earth.

▲ The Shri Vishwanath Temple is one of the most famous of Varanasi's 23,000 Hindu temples.

However, there is more to Varanasi than religion. For centuries the Grand Trunk Road was a major trade route. Spices, silks and other goods were transported from east to west along this ancient road. Varanasi has a long history of making beautiful silks, muslins and perfumes, and today silk weaving and textile manufacturing are still important industries for the economy of the city.

▲ The River Ganges is used by millions of people every day all along its course.

River tour

All along the riverbank are long sets of steps leading down to the river. These are called *ghats*. Some are used by bathers; others are where dead bodies are cremated. You can explore them by foot or hire a rowing boat. Early in the morning is the best time to go, when the city is just waking up. But remember, the Ganges is a very special place for Hindus and visitors should treat it with respect. You must ask before you walk on to some of the ghats, and you may not be allowed near a cremation unless you are a Hindu. The Ganges is India's longest river, rising in the Himalayas and flowing 2,525 km to the Bay of Bengal.

Sarnath

About 10 km north-east of Varanasi lies the ancient city of Sarnath. You can reach it easily by auto rickshaw. Sarnath is a sacred place for Buddhists. It is where the Buddha gave his first sermon in the 6th century BCE. Look out for the remains of the Dhamekh Stupa, a burial mound encased in stone that stands on the spot where the Buddha taught. There is also a fantastic museum here with lots of Buddhist treasures on display.

Hinduism

More than three quarters of Indians are Hindus. Most believe in a 'Great Soul' whose powers are represented by different gods and goddesses. Hindus also believe in reincarnation – when a person's soul is reborn in a different body when he or she dies. What your next life is depends on how well or badly you have behaved in this one. This is called *karma*.

▲ Buddhist monks at the Dhamekh Stupa.

19

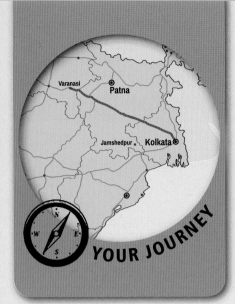

YOUR JOURNEY

VARANASI TO KOLKATA

Head to Mughalsarai railway station just outside Varanasi to catch the sleeper train to Kolkata. You'll leave in the early evening and arrive in the morning, so book a bunk and pack a picnic. You can also buy little clay cups of *chai* (hot, sweet tea) from the tea-sellers at the stations along the way. On arrival at Kolkata's enormous Howrah Station, you can take a taxi into the city, crossing the Hoogly River over the famous Howrah Bridge.

About Kolkata

Around 14.5 million people live in Kolkata, India's second biggest city after Mumbai. Kolkata is an extraordinary place. It has historic buildings, delicious food, world-famous cricket, crowded markets and brand new shopping malls. Here, you can see many sides of Indian life, with people sleeping on the streets right next to luxury apartment blocks.

Kolkata is also a city of culture. It is the centre of education in east India and a hub for the arts and literature. To get around the city, you can walk, take the Metro (the first one to be built in India) or hop on a tram, bus or cycle rickshaw.

▶ You can find Kolkata's daily flower market at the eastern end of the Howrah Bridge.

▶ The Victoria Memorial is built from the same type of white marble as the Taj Mahal.

Famous landmarks

Kolkata was the capital of the British Raj and many buildings remain from that time. One of the city's most famous landmarks is the Victoria Memorial. It is a memorial to the British Queen Victoria (1819–1901), who was also the Empress of India during the Raj. It was completed in 1921.

Around the Victoria Memorial is a huge park called the Maidan. This is where people come to play cricket and football, take their daily walks and even graze their animals. It has also been the venue for many political meetings and rallies, and book fairs.

Cricket mad

Cricket is the most popular sport in India, especially in Kolkata. Everywhere you go, you see people playing cricket in the streets and on playing fields. The city is home to Eden Gardens, one of the most famous cricket stadiums in the world. The stadium can hold almost 70,000 people and is always packed for national and international matches. It's an experience not to be missed – if you can manage to obtain a ticket!

▲ Indian cricketer Sachin Tendulkar leaves the field after an international match against England. He is regarded as one of the greatest cricketers of all time.

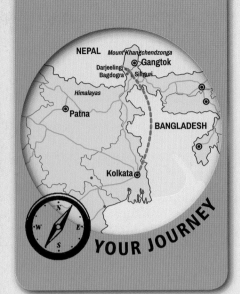

YOUR JOURNEY

KOLKATA TO DARJEELING

From Kolkata, hop on to another plane for the short flight to Siliguri in the north-east. You are leaving the big city behind and heading into another world via the DHR (Darjeeling Himalayan Railway) to the beautiful hill station of Darjeeling. Nestling among the foothills of the mighty Himalaya Mountains, Darjeeling has a truly spectacular location. There are snow-capped peaks to marvel at, Buddhist monasteries to visit and refreshing Darjeeling tea to sip. Try to plan your visit for spring or autumn when the weather is dry and warm – winters can get very cold.

◀ The DHR takes passengers up through the mountains to Darjeeling.

From Tiger Hill, the views of Khangchendzonga (8,586 m), the highest peak in India and the third highest on Earth, are spectacular.

Toy Train

The DHR chugs its way up to Darjeeling, zig-zagging as it climbs the hillside. Nicknamed the 'Toy Train', its steam locomotives first ran in 1881. Today, the train line is a UNESCO World Heritage Site. You used to be able to travel directly from Siliguri to Darjeeling but landslides (which are common in India) have destroyed part of the track. Instead, catch the train at Kurseong, a short drive from Siliguri. There are two trains a day to Darjeeling, and the trip takes around 3 hours.

Mountain views

The Himalayas were formed when the Indo-Australian and the Eurasian tectonic plates collided, 50 million years ago. The collision caused the rock to be folded into massive peaks. A stunning way to see the Himalayas is to get up early and take a jeep from Darjeeling to a viewpoint, called Tiger Hill. If you're keen to do some serious trekking, try the five-day Singalila Ridge Trek from Darjeeling. It's a tough walk so you'll need to be fit, but it's worth it for the breathtaking views.

Time for tea

Darjeeling is famous for its tea, which should be drunk black or with a slice of lemon. The tea grown in Darjeeling is a Chinese type, rather than Assam – the Indian type mostly drunk in India. Tea plantations surround the town and are fascinating places to visit. Take a tour of the Happy Valley Tea Estate. A guide will show you around the factory and you'll see the tea leaves being dried, rolled and processed.

The tea is picked by hand as the delicate tea leaves need careful handling.

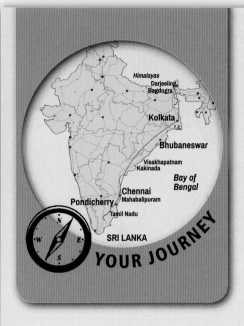

YOUR JOURNEY

DARJEELING TO CHENNAI

Your next stop is Chennai, more than 2,000 km to the south. To cover this long distance, head for Bagdogra, the nearest airport to Darjeeling. From there, you fly to Kolkata, then on to Chennai, the capital of the state of Tamil Nadu, famous for its stunning coastline, historic Hindu temples and delicious food.

About Chennai

Until the arrival of the British in the 17th century, Chennai was a group of villages nestling among the rice fields. The British set up a trading post, which grew into a thriving city. Today, Chennai makes a handy starting place for a tour of southern India but it's worth having a look around the city before you set off. Take a stroll along Marina Beach or take an auto rickshaw to Fort St George, the headquarters of the historic British East India Company, which is now one of the oldest museums in the country.

▼ Families enjoy socialising on Marina Beach. Few people swim in the sea here, as the currents are dangerously strong.

▲ One of the tallest of the 14 gateway towers at the Meenakshi Amman Temple.

Temple tour

Tamil Nadu is home to some of the greatest Hindu temples in India. Special temple tours run from Chennai, by luxury coach. Don't miss the extraordinary Meenakshi Amman Temple in Madurai, dedicated to the god, Shiva. The entrances to the temple are 14 towering gateways, called *gopurams*. These are covered in thousands of brightly coloured figures of gods, goddesses, demons and heroes.

Modern Chennai

Today, Chennai is the most visited city in India. This well-connected city has the biggest port in the Bay of Bengal and is an international hub for shipping. Many banks are also located here, including a branch of the World Bank. But it's not all serious business in Chennai, as people here tend to be a bit more laid back than in other large Indian cities. Many take part in water sports along the coast or have fun in the nearby amusement parks.

South Indian food

If all that sightseeing is making you hungry, stop off for some typical south Indian food, which is traditionally served on a banana leaf.

Dosa – rice pancake, served with spicy potatoes

Uttapam – thick, spicy pancake, served with onions

Idli – spongy rice cakes

Rasam – hot and sour tamarind soup

Sambar – lentil soup

▲ A selection of traditional south Indian foods.

▲ New cars lined up for export at Chennai Port.

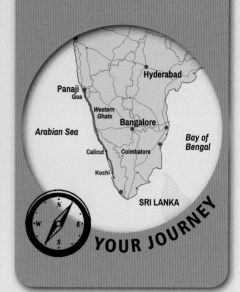

KOCHI TO GOA

For the last stage of your journey, catch a train from Kochi and head up the west coast to Goa. Look for the Western Ghats on your way – a mountain range that runs parallel to the west coast. After all that sightseeing, it's time for a well-earned rest. Goa is India's smallest state and is famous for its beautiful beaches and relaxed way of life. Portuguese traders settled here in 1510, and Goa remained under Portuguese rule for the next 450 years.

Panaji

Panaji is the capital of Goa, located at the mouth of the Mandovi river. Take a stroll through the Old Town, a tangle of narrow streets, lined with traditional Portuguese-style houses, and cafes and bakeries, selling Portuguese delicacies, such as *bebinca* (cake). Some of the older people here still speak Portuguese although the main language spoken is Konkani (not Hindi). In the evening, catch a boat from Mandovi bridge for a sunset cruise along the Mandovi river.

▲ These colourful buildings with their tiled roofs are typical of Goa's Portuguese style.

Old Goa

A short rickshaw ride from Panaji is the old Portuguese capital of Old Goa. The Portuguese settlers were Roman Catholics and many Goans still follow the Christian faith. Old Goa is packed with historic churches and monasteries, many of which are still in use. Start your tour at the magnificent Basilica of Bom Jesus, famous for the tomb of Saint Francis Xavier, Goa's patron saint. Then head to Sé Cathedral, believed to be Asia's biggest church. Look out for the huge golden bell, and the enormous gilded screen behind the altar.

▶ The gilded screen inside Sé Cathedral.

Goan cuisine

End your Indian adventure with one final meal. Goan food is a delicious mixture of Indian and Portuguese flavours. Traditional dishes include vindaloo, a dish made with pork, marinaded in garlic and vinegar, with fiery red chillies added. It is very spicy and very hot, so make sure you have plenty of water or lassi handy! Fish is also very popular. A typical lunch might be fried mackerel, cooked in coconut milk, and served with rice.

◀ Prawn vindaloo is another Goan speciality.

Beach life

Goa has more than 100 km of beaches, attracting thousands of tourists every year. One of the most popular beaches is Colva in south Goa. Backed by shady palm trees, you can jump in a boat and go dolphin watching, or simply relax, soak up the sun and watch the local fishermen haul up their catch.

GLOSSARY

alpine
A high mountain habitat.

architect
A person who designs buildings and supervises how they are built.

astronomical
Something that is connected to astronomy, the study of the stars, planets and space.

backwater
Part of a river with little or no current.

boulevard
A wide, tree-lined road in a city.

British Raj
The time between 1858 and 1947 when India was ruled by Great Britain.

Buddha
The founder of the Buddhist religion, believed to have lived either c.563–483 BCE or c.480–400 BCE.

Buddhist
A follower of the religion of Buddhism, based on the teachings of Buddha.

cremated
When a body is burned to ashes, after someone has died.

democracy
A country that is governed by ministers who are elected by the people of the country.

ecological
The way something is done that is good for the environment, or does very little harm.

epic poems
Long poems which tell the story of the lives and actions of gods and heroes of legend.

floodplain
The flat land around a river, made up of soil deposited when the river floods.

foothills
Low hills at the base of a mountain.

gilded
Something that is covered in gold.

granary
A region that produces a large amount of grain; a place where grain is stored.

Indus Valley Civilisation
A Bronze Age civilisation that flourished around the Indus river, which runs through what is now Pakistan, northern India and Tibet.

Mughals
Muslim emperors from the north-west of India who ruled India from the 16th to 18th centuries.

monsoon
A seasonal change of weather that includes high rainfall and a change in wind direction.

murals
Large paintings on walls.

muslins
Fine pieces of cloth made from cotton.

observatory
A building where people can observe and study the weather and space.

patron saint
A saint that is special to a country, place or group of people.

pilgrims
People who make a special journey to a place that is sacred to their religion.

plantations
Huge farms or estates where crops, such as tea, rubber and coffee, are grown.

promontory
A high point of rocky land that juts out into the sea.

republic
A country which has a president as its head of state.

rickshaw
A small, two-wheeled vehicle, powered by an engine or a man riding a bicycle.

Indian rupee
The official currency of the Republic of India.

sacred
Something that is important or special to a particular religion.

slum
An area of overcrowded housing that is in very poor condition.

sub-continent
A large area of land that is a distinct part of a continent.

sundial
A device used to tell the time during the day, using the length of shadows.

synagogue
A place where Jewish people go to worship.

temperate
A climate that has mild temperatures.

tamarind
The fruit of an evergreen tree, used as food and to make drinks and medicines.

tectonic plates
The huge pieces of the Earth's crust which carry the continents.

tributary
A stream or river that feeds another, larger one.

BOOKS TO READ

Lonely Planet India (Travel Guide) by Sarina Singh (Lonely Planet, 2013)

Eyewitness Travel Guide: India (Dorling Kindersley, 2014)

The Rough Guide to India by Emma Boyle (Rough Guides, 2013)

Eyewitness Top 10 Travel Guide: Delhi (Dorling Kindersley, 2014)

Lonely Planet South India and Kerala by Sarina Singh (Lonely Planet, 2013)

Languages of the World: Hindi by Anita Ganeri (Raintree, 2012)

Countries Around the World: India by Ali Brownlie Bojang (Raintree, 2012)

Developing World: India and Mumbai by Jenny Vaughan (Franklin Watts, 2016)

WEBSITES

http://www.roughguides.com/destinations/asia/india/

This Rough Guide website is packed with interesting and useful information for your visit. There are tips on where and when to travel, things to see and not to miss, and ideas for lots of great intineraries to inspire your own journey around India.

http://www.lonelyplanet.com/india

Lonely Planet's website is a great introduction to India, and tells you about the best places to visit, historical and geographical information, food and drink to sample, and practical hints and tips about money, health, language and local customs.

http://travel.michelin.com/web/destination/India

This website from Michelin provides all the information you'll need for a fascinating and safe journey around India. Follow some alternative travel routes, take your pick from loads of travel activities and check out the best places to stay.

https://www.gov.uk/foreign-travel-advice/india

It's always a good idea to check out the official government advice before you make any journey abroad. You can find out the latest news and information about India on this UK government website.

Note to parents and teachers:
Every effort has been made by the Publishers to ensure that the websites in this book are suitable for children, that they are of the highest educational value, and that they contain no inappropriate or offensive material. However, because of the nature of the Internet, it is impossible to guarantee that the contents of these sites will not be altered. We strongly advise that Internet access is supervised by a responsible adult.

INDEX